P9-CFZ-290

Holidays

KWANZAA

By Deborah M. Newton Chocolate

Illustrations by Melodye Rosales

CP CHILDRENS PRESS®

CHICAGO

Library of Congress Cataloging-in-Publication Data

Chocolate, Deborah Newton.
  Kwanzaa / by Deborah Newton Chocolate ; illustrated by Melodye
Rosales.
    p.   cm.
  Summary: Discusses the holiday in which Afro-Americans celebrate
their roots and cultural heritage from Africa.
  ISBN 0-516-03991-1
  1. Kwanzaa—Juvenile literature. 2. Afro-Americans—Social life
and customs—Juvenile literature. [1. Kwanzaa. 2. Afro-Americans—
Social life and customs.] I. Rosales, Melodye, ill. II. Title.
GT4403.C46 1990   89-25418
394.2'68—dc20   CIP
                                                  AC

For my husband Bob,
one of the *watu wazuri*,
with love   —DMC

INTRODUCTION

Africa is a big continent. Many different African tribes live in Africa and they have many different customs and beliefs. But all African people know that the fruits of the earth bring life to them. The earth nourishes them, so Africans say that the earth is their mother. Africans have always celebrated planting and harvest, but even more important to Africans are the spirits of their ancestors. At harvesttime, Africans offer the first fruits of the harvest to those who have gone before them.

The different tribes of Africa speak a variety of languages. The Swahili, or *kiswahili*, language is spoken over a wider area of Africa than any other language. Many tribal groups speak Swahili and their own language too, especially tribes living along the eastern shore of Africa.

NIA · KUUMBA · IMANI

KUJICHAGULIA

UMOJA

Matunde ya kwanza (mah-TOON-day yah KWAHN-zah)

The holiday name *Kwanzaa* comes from the East African Swahili word *kwanza*, meaning "the first." *Matunde ya kwanza* is a Swahili phrase meaning "the first fruits." The extra "a" in the Kwanzaa holiday name gives the word seven letters, one letter for each of the seven principles in the Kwanzaa value system.

Kwanzaa celebrates kinship and gathering, or reunion. It celebrates the ties that bind African harvest customs to the cultural and social history of African-Americans. Even though tribal ceremonies may no longer be performed in modern-day Africa, the beliefs and values behind them are important to Africa's past and present. And they are also important to African-American people.

UJIMA · UJAMMA

Harambee (hah-RAHM-bee)

There are many ways to celebrate Kwanzaa, just as there are many ways to celebrate any holiday. This book about Kwanzaa is also a book about family. I have written it so that boys and girls, especially those of African-American origin, may share the good feeling that comes from celebrating and honoring the ties that bind people to the spirits of their ancestors.

Harambee!

Deborah M. Newton Chocolate

THE SEVEN PRINCIPLES OF KWANZAA

umoja (oo-MO-jah), unity.
kujichagulia (koo-jee-cha-goo-LEE-ah), self-determination.
ujima (oo-JEE-mah), collective work and responsibility.
ujamma (oo-JAH-mah), cooperative economics.
nia (NEE-ah), purpose.
kuumba (koo-OOM-bah), creativity.
imani (ee-MAH-nee), faith.

Every year, from the day after Christmas until the first day of the new year, our family celebrates Kwanzaa!

Kwanzaa is an African-American celebration. The name comes from the East African Swahili word *kwanza*, meaning "the first." Kwanzaa is a gathering time, just like Thanksgiving or a family reunion.

Many of our ancestors were farmers. The seven principles of Kwanzaa celebrate African harvesttime and a way of life handed down to us by our ancestors and parents.

lappa (LAH-pah)
buba (BOO-bah)
dashiki (dah-SHEE-kee)
kanzus (KAHN-zus)
kofis (KOO-fees)
bendera (ben-DER-ah)
karamu (kah-RAH-mu)

In keeping with the spirit of Kwanzaa, Mama wears a *lappa* or *buba*, which is an African dress. She braids her hair into beautiful cornrows.

Daddy and Allen and I wear *dashikis* or *kanzus*. This is traditional dress for African men. We wear *kofis* on our heads and beads around our necks.

We decorate our home in the black, red, and green colors of Kwanzaa. We fly our *bendera*, or flag. Black is for the color of our people. Red is for our continuing struggle. And green is for the lush, rolling hills of our beautiful motherland, Africa. Green also is the color of hope, represented by African-American children. Together we prepare a table for the Kwanzaa *karamu*, or feast.

mkeka (m-KAY-kah)
kinara (kee-NAH-rah)
mishumaa saba (mee-SHOO-mah SAH-bah)

Mama puts a *mkeke,* or straw mat, on the table. Aunt Ife wove it for the celebration. In Africa it is an old custom to make things by hand. The handwoven mkeke stands for our past.

On top of the mkeke, Daddy puts a *kinara* or candle holder. The kinara is the holder of the flame. It stands for all black people, both past and present. The *mishumaa saba,* or seven candles in the kinara, stand for the seven Kwanzaa principles that teach us how to live.

mazao (mah-ZAH-oo)
vibunzi (vee-BOON-zee)
zawadi (zah-WAH-dee)

Allen places a basket filled with *mazao*, or crops, on the table. It is a symbol of the African harvest and thanksgiving. We gather with our relatives to give thanks just as our ancestors did.

I put *vibunzi*, or ears of corn, on the table. The ears of corn stand for the number of children in the home. Our table has two ears of corn.

We show our love for our family through the *zawadi*, or gifts, we make. On the night before the last day of Kwanzaa, we give our parents gifts that remind us of Africa and our African-American ancestors. Allen and I earn our gifts by keeping the promises we made in the past year.

harambee (hah-RAHM-bee)
nguzo saba (n-GOO-zoo SAH-bah)
umoja (oo-MO-jah)

Each day, from sunrise to sunset, we
do not eat. In the evening we gather in a
circle around the karamu table. We share
our home and food with family and
friends, just as our ancestors shared the
fruits of the hunt and the harvest.

Each night a candle is lit and one of
the seven Kwanzaa principles is recited.
On the first day of Kwanzaa, Daddy
lights the black candle in the center of
the kinara.

"Harambee!" he says.

"Harambee!" we answer. He recites
the first principle of the *nguzo saba*, the
seven principles of Kwanzaa. "*Umoja*
means unity," says Daddy. "On this first
day of Kwanzaa, let us remember the
importance of unity in the family. Let us
love one another and stand up for one
another. Let us honor our ancestors by
celebrating our past."

We pass the *kikombe cha umoja*, or
unity cup. We pour a libation, an
offering to the memory of our ancestors,
in the direction of the four winds—
north, south, east, and west. And then,
to honor our ancestors and in the spirit
of unity, each person takes a sip.
  The delicious aromas of collard greens

kikombe cha umoja
(kee-KOOM-bay CHA oo-MO-jah)

simmering in sweet meat, black-eyed peas, and buttermilk cornbread mean it is time for the first karamu, or feast. We eat black-eyed peas for good luck and greens for prosperity. There are platters of fried chicken and baked catfish. For dessert, there is sweet potato pie, peach cobbler, rice pudding, and carrot cake.

Mufaro, a cousin, and Allen and I
play congas. The rhythm is a heartbeat
that brings everyone to their feet.
Everyone dances to the music we make.

kujichagulia (koo-jee-cha-goo-LEE-ah)
kikombe (kee-KOOM-bay)

On the second day of Kwanzaa, Uncle Buddy lights a red candle in the kinara. "Always do the right thing," says Uncle Buddy. "Always stand up for what is right. This is what *kujichagulia*, or self-determination, means."

Uncle Buddy passes the *kikombe*, or cup. He recalls the days when he was a boy living on a sharecropping farm down south. He tells us stories about our grandfathers. He remembers the name of the village in Africa where his great-great grandmother was born.

"Habari gani?" ("What's the news?")
greets Mama.

"Ujima!" everyone answers.

"Today I light the third candle of
Kwanzaa for ujima!"

The glow from the flame dances
across Mama's dark face. Shadows fill
the room. Mama takes an ear of corn
from the basket. "Ujima stands for
collective work and responsibility. "Our
corn," she explains, "reminds us of the
harvest that comes from ujima. Without
work, there is no reward, no harvest for
our people."

A family photo album, a cane-bottomed basket, a flatiron, and a set of wedding rings are some of the things that have been handed down in our family from generation to generation. We hear the story that goes with each of them. There is a top hat that belonged to my great-great grandfather, and a feathered headband that belonged to my great-great grandmother. Our great-great grandparents once sang and danced in traveling stage shows across the South.

Mufaro stands behind the kinara and lights the candle for the fourth celebration day, a red one, for *ujamma*. "Ujamma means 'cooperative economics.' My family honors ujamma by helping me finish school. When I become a doctor, I'll come back to the community and help out."

Nia means "purpose." On the fifth

26

ujima (oo-JEE-mah)

day, I light a green candle. I greet
everyone with, "Harambee!"

"Harambee!" they answer.

"I have a purpose, no matter how
small. My purpose is to keep promises
and to honor my ancestors and
parents." Both Mama and Daddy give
me a great big hug after the kikombe cha
umoja is passed around.

27

On New Year's Eve we celebrate the sixth principle of Kwanzaa, which is *kuumba*, or creativity. We work on the gifts we will exchange. There is more music and song and dance. Some of the music is African and some of it is African-American. Cousin Ebon plays a thumb piano. Uncle Will dances a cakewalk to it.

Later that evening, we present our gifts. Allen and I give Mama a tie-dyed red, black, and green *gele*, or head wrap, made in art class. For Daddy we have a hand-carved flute.

Mama and Daddy surprise us with pocket watches that once belonged to our grandfathers.

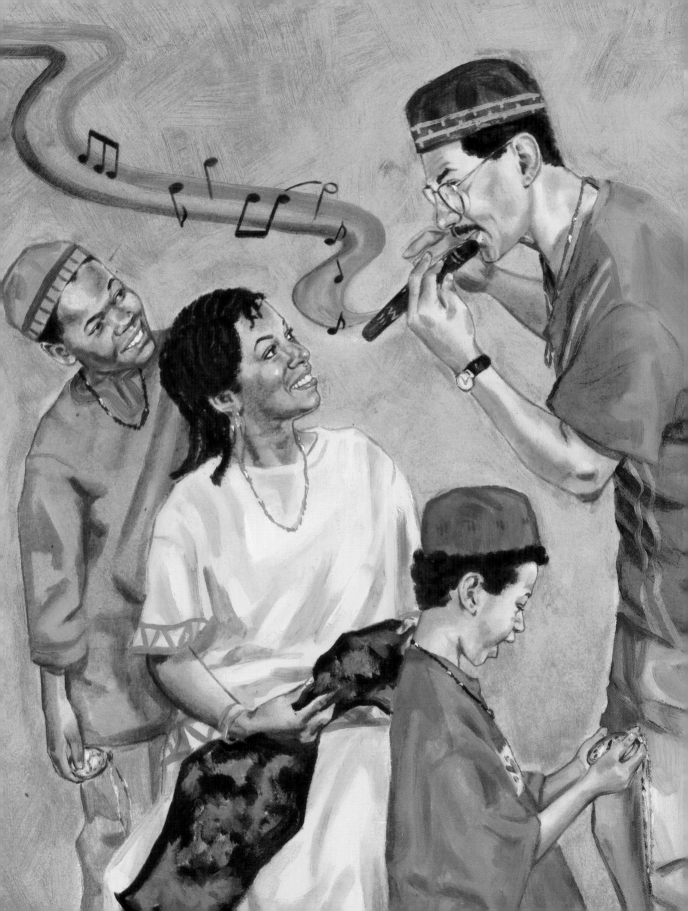

imani (ee-MAH-nee)

After midnight, in the early morning of New Year's Day, Grandma Lela lights the last candle in honor of Kwanzaa. She recites the principle of *imani*, which means "faith." "It is up to us to keep the faith of our ancestors. We must always stand together and be strong." She talks about Sojourner Truth and Dr. Martin Luther King, Jr. "Let imani burn as a flame in our hearts in the coming year," Grandma says. "Let it light our way until we gather to celebrate this time next year."

Nelson Mandela
Mary Francis Berry Barbara Jordan   Harriet Tubman
Shirley Chisholm   Medgar Evers

Steve Biko

Rosa Parks

Sojourner Truth   Marcus Garvey   Martin Luther King Jr.

31

About the Author

Deborah M. Newton Chocolate is a Chicago writer. She is a graduate of Spelman College and Brown University. As the mother of Bobby and Allen, and as a former editor of children's books, she brings a special sensitivity to her writing. She lives on Chicago's west side with her husband, Bob, and her two school-age children. This is her first book.

About the Artist

Melodye Rosales has been a children's illustrator for many years. However, this story brought special meaning to her. As a black artist this was her first opportunity to do a body of work in which she was able to illustrate a book dedicated entirely to a black experience.
After studying at the University of Illinois Urbana campus, Columbia College, and the School of the Art Institute, Melodye became a wife and mother of two. They all reside in Chicago, Illinois.